DISCARD

Breaking Barriers

Athletes Who Led the Way

by

Joanne and James Mattern

Perfection Learning®

Cover Design: Michelle Glass
Inside Design: Tobi Cunningham

About the Authors

Joanne Mattern is the author of many books for children. She especially likes writing nonfiction because it allows her to bring real people, places, and events to life. "I firmly believe that everything in the world is a story waiting to be told."

Along with writing, Joanne enjoys speaking to school and community groups about the topics in her books. She is also a huge baseball fan and enjoys music and needlework.

Joanne's husband, James, enjoys all sports. He is especially interested in sports history, trivia, and statistics.

Joanne and James live in the Hudson Valley of New York State with their young daughter. The family also includes a greyhound and two cats, and "more animals are always welcome!"

Image Credits: arttoday.com pp. 5 (bottom), 7, 8, 10–11, 13, 14 (bottom), 15, 16, 18–19, 21, 22, 23 (bottom), 24, 25, 26, 27, 28, 29 (bottom), 30, 31, 32–33, 34, 36 (bottom), 37, 38, 39, 41, 42, 43 (bottom), 44, 45, 46–47, 48, 49, 50 (background), 51 (bottom), 52, 53 (top), 53 (bottom), 55, 58; Library of Congress pp. 5 (top), 6, 9, 12; Associated Press pp. 14 (top), 17, 20, 23 (top), 29 (top), 35, 36 (top), 40, 43 (top), 50 (foreground), 51 (top), 54, 56, 57

Printed in the United States of America. For information, contact
Perfection Learning® Corporation, 1000 North Second Avenue,
P.O. Box 500, Logan, Iowa 51546-0500
perfectionlearning.com
Tel: 1-800-831-4190 • Fax: 1-712-644-2392

Paperback ISBN 0-7891-5534-6
Cover Craft® ISBN 0-7569-0305-x
2 3 4 5 6 7 PP 08 07 06 05 04 03

Table of Contents

Introduction

Succeeding in sports is hard work. Athletes face many challenges during their careers. Some have to overcome injuries or other setbacks. Some have to learn to work with their teammates.

But in the past some athletes faced even more difficult challenges than just winning a game. They had to overcome **obstacles** based on their color, their **gender**, or their abilities. For years, blacks and women were not welcome to compete with white men in most sports. And disabled athletes have always faced **barriers** to success.

Today, most sports are open to all, regardless of their background. We often take for granted that everyone has an equal chance in sports. But that opportunity wouldn't exist if it weren't for the sacrifices and hard work of sports pioneers.

Who were the men and women who broke the barriers of color, gender, and ability? In this book, you'll meet six special athletes and one special **league** that changed sports forever and helped open the doors to all.

Jackie Robinson

April 15, 1947, was no ordinary day in bascball history. On that day, Jackie Robinson appeared in his first major league game. He was the first baseman for the Brooklyn Dodgers.

What was so unusual about a **rookie** joining a baseball team? Jackie Robinson was black. And until that day, every major league baseball player had been white. On April 15, 1947, Robinson changed baseball—and history—forever.

Jack Roosevelt Robinson was born on January 31, 1919, in Cairo, Georgia. He was the youngest of five children. Robinson's grandparents had been slaves. His parents were free. But their lives were far from easy. The Robinsons were sharecroppers. That meant that they lived in a house owned by a white farmer. The Robinsons had to pay the owner to farm the land, to live in the house, and to buy supplies. After paying for all those things, they hardly had any money left.

When Robinson was growing up, he faced a great deal of **discrimination**. In those days, the southern United States was **segregated**. That meant that blacks and whites had to do most things separately.

Black and white children went to separate schools. Schools for black children weren't as good as the schools white children attended. Black students had to use old books. Their teachers often had little training. Sometimes the schools had no heat or water.

Blacks were not allowed to eat in certain restaurants. They had to sit in special seats or sections on trains and buses. They weren't allowed to vote or own property. In almost every area of life, they were treated as if they were not as good as white people.

Robinson's father left the family when his children were very young. A few years later, Robinson's mother, Mallie, moved the family to California. Her brother lived there. He had told Mallie that the family could have a better life in California.

There wasn't as much segregation in California as in Georgia. But the Robinsons still lived in poverty.

Mallie and her children moved in with her brother. Thirteen people crowded into the small, three-room apartment with no hot water or electricity. There was barely enough food to feed everyone.

Later, Robinson's mother got a job as a cleaning lady. In time, she was able to buy her own home. Some of the Robinsons' white neighbors were not happy about a black family living on their street. But Mallie Robinson refused to back down.

Jackie Robinson later wrote that his mother "never lost her composure. She didn't allow us to go out of our way to **antagonize** the whites, and she still made it perfectly clear to us and to them that she was not at all afraid of them and that she had no intention of allowing them to mistreat us." Despite a hard life, Robinson's family was close and loving.

Robinson did well in school. But he really stood out in sports. He played soccer, baseball, football, basketball, and tennis.

Robinson discovered that sports was one area where he was free to compete with whites. He was such a talented athlete that the other children didn't care about the color of his skin. They just wanted Robinson to play on their teams! Robinson even played with children who were much older and bigger than he was.

Robinson wasn't good at just one sport. He was great at all of them! He played on his high school's baseball, football, track, and basketball teams. When he went on to Pasadena Junior College and the University of California at Los Angeles (UCLA), he continued to play different sports. He helped his teams win in every one of them.

Robinson enjoyed college. But he wasn't able to finish his education. His family needed money. So Robinson left UCLA during his senior year to work as a coach.

In 1942, Robinson was drafted into the U.S. Army. At that time, the army was segregated. Robinson was angry that blacks and whites were not treated equally. He fought for—and won—the right to attend Officers' Candidate School.

But Robinson was not allowed to join the army's all-white baseball team. He even quit the football team when he and other blacks were not allowed to play in a game because the opposing team complained.

Robinson's final army battle came on a bus. The government had banned segregated seating on base buses. Still, Robinson was asked to move to the back of a bus at Fort Hood in Texas.

When Robinson refused to move, he was arrested. He was charged with conduct unbecoming an officer. Robinson was later cleared of the charge. But he'd had enough of army life. In 1944, he asked for an honorable **discharge** and left the armed forces.

In 1945 when he was 26 years old, Robinson joined the Kansas City Monarchs. This baseball team was part of the Negro leagues. Because blacks could not play in the major leagues, they had formed their own baseball leagues.

Robinson was a terrific player. But

he didn't enjoy life in the Negro leagues. Players often had to stay in run-down hotels and eat in shabby restaurants. "White" businesses refused to serve blacks. Most of all, Robinson missed playing on teams with the best players, both white and black.

Then on August 28, 1945, Jackie Robinson met Branch Rickey, and Robinson's life changed forever. Rickey was the general manager of a major league team, the Brooklyn Dodgers. He wanted to bring black players into the major leagues.

Rickey had two reasons for wanting to add black players. First, Rickey knew that black players would make the Dodgers a better team. Then more fans would come to the ballpark. As a result, Rickey would make more money.

But Rickey had a more important reason. He felt racial discrimination was wrong. He wanted to do something to end it.

Rickey knew that many people would be against having black players in the major leagues. So he kept his plans secret. He told everyone that he was starting a team called the Brooklyn Brown Dodgers in a new Negro league. That allowed him to talk to black players without anyone discovering what he really had in mind.

During his search, Rickey heard a lot of good things about Jackie Robinson's ability and attitude. After he saw Robinson play, Rickey knew he wanted him for the Dodgers. He asked Robinson if he would be willing to break baseball's color barrier. He warned Robinson that he would be insulted and attacked by players and fans who didn't want blacks to play major league baseball. He also told Robinson that he expected him to play hard and ignore any abuse he faced.

"I want a player with guts enough *not* to fight back," Rickey reportedly told Robinson. Robinson said he was glad Rickey was willing to take this chance. And he promised there would be no incidents between him and anyone who abused him because of the color of his skin.

At first, Robinson played for the Montreal Royals. The Royals were a minor league team owned by the Dodgers. Robinson played for the Royals during the 1946 season.

During that time, Robinson led the league in batting with a .349 average and in fielding with a .985 average. He also scored 113 runs. Most importantly, Robinson handled the pressures of being the only black player in the league with dignity and grace. Now it was time to move up to the majors.

At first, some of

Robinson's new teammates on the Brooklyn Dodgers didn't want him on the team. They passed around a **petition** demanding he stay off the team. But Branch Rickey refused to back down.

Most of the Dodgers welcomed Robinson to the team. One of his teammates, Pee Wee Reese, even made a public display of his support. During a game when Robinson was being **taunted** by the fans, Reese walked up to Robinson on the field and put his arm around him. This gesture showed the world that he would stand by his teammate.

Robinson didn't just face taunts and insults. He also faced physical danger. Fans threw things at him when he was on the field. Players on other teams spat at him and tried to spike him with their shoes. Pitchers threw fastballs at his head. Robinson even received death threats.

But no matter what happened, Robinson refused to show any anger or fear. Instead, he played the best baseball he could. During the 1947 season, Robinson led the National League with 29 stolen bases. Sportswriters admired both his courage and his athletic ability. At the end of the season, they named him Rookie of the Year.

Robinson played first and second base for the Dodgers for ten years. His career batting average was .311. He led the Dodgers to six World Series appearances. He helped them win the championship in 1955.

Robinson retired from baseball in 1956. He was voted into the Baseball Hall of Fame in 1962.

After he retired from baseball, Robinson became the president of a large company. He also worked for the Civil Rights movement to bring equal treatment to black people.

Robinson started the Freedom National Bank in New York City's Harlem. This bank was owned and run by black people and brought business opportunities to the black community.

Jackie Robinson died on October 24, 1972.

Jackie Robinson was a great baseball player. But he achieved much more. Robinson opened the door for other black athletes. By 1959, all major league baseball teams had at least one black player.

Today, black athletes are common in most sports. Jackie Robinson's accomplishments were felt outside of sports too. He helped the world see that the color of a person's skin had nothing to do with his or her accomplishments in life.

Blacks in Other Sports

Jackie Robinson broke baseball's color barrier. Who were the first blacks in other major sports?

- Kenny Washington signed with the Los Angeles Rams in 1946. He was the first black to play in the National Football League (NFL) in modern times. Blacks had played on several teams during the early days of football before the NFL was formed.

- Earl Lloyd became the first black American to play in the National Basketball Association (NBA) on October 31, 1950. He played for the Washington Capitols.

- Hockey was the last major team sport to **integrate**. Willie O'Ree played his first game for the Boston Bruins on January 18, 1958.

Billie Jean King

2

It was 1967, and Billie Jean King was angry. She had recently won the women's **singles** championship at Wimbledon in England and at the U.S. National **Tournament** (now called the U.S. Open). She was the best women's tennis player in the world.

But none of this mattered to King. She was sick and tired of the unequal treatment women tennis players received. So she decided to do something about it.

Billie Jean Moffitt was always determined to get her way. She was born on November 22, 1943, in Long Beach, California. As a child, she loved sports. She spent her days playing softball, basketball, and football with the other kids in the neighborhood. One day, she told her mother she would do something great in the sports world.

Mr. and Mrs. Moffitt didn't like the idea of their daughter playing football. So when Billie Jean was 11 years old, they suggested she take up tennis.

Her parents didn't have enough money to buy her a racket, so Billie Jean did odd jobs around the neighborhood to earn money. Once she'd bought her racket, she started taking lessons on Long Beach's public courts.

Billie Jean Moffitt didn't look like a tennis player. Instead of being graceful and having long legs and arms, she was short and pudgy. She couldn't see the ball unless she was wearing thick glasses. She didn't even wear a dress like the other girls. Instead, she wore shorts and a T-shirt.

Billie Jean didn't act like a tennis player either. Tennis players were supposed to be quiet. But Billie Jean talked to herself while she played. If she won a point, she let out a whoop. If she did something wrong, she yelled at herself. No one in Long Beach had ever seen a tennis player like this before!

Billie Jean may have looked odd, but she certainly could play tennis. By 1958 when she was 15, she was one of the highest-ranked tennis players in California. Soon after that, she ranked fifth in the country for girls 15 and under. By the age of 17, she ranked fourth among all U.S. women.

Billie Jean played in her first Wimbledon tournament when she was 17 years old. The tournament is played in England. It is one of the most important competitions in tennis. She lost in the first round of the singles tournament. But she and her partner, Karen Hantze, surprised everyone by winning the **doubles** tournament.

Despite her athletic ability, no colleges offered Billie Jean a

scholarship. Women couldn't make enough money to support themselves playing tennis **professionally** in those days. So Billie Jean became a part-time tennis player. During the fall and winter, she worked and attended college. In the spring and summer, she played tennis.

By 1965, Billie Jean had married and changed her name to Billie Jean King. Now she was ready to play tennis all year long. Billie Jean had completed school and was ready to earn a living playing tennis full-time.

In 1967, King was named Athlete of the Year by the Associated Press. By 1968, she had won three Wimbledon titles, the U.S. Nationals, and the Australian Open championship. King was now the most commanding women's tennis player. She was

ranked first in the world.

King was very successful. But she had to work as a tennis instructor to earn $32 a week to make ends meet. Meanwhile, her husband worked in a factory.

King felt that there were a lot of things wrong with women's tennis. She was angry that top-ranked players received huge sums of money to appear in tournaments. These players received that money even if they lost in the first round. It was also unfair that there were no cash prizes given to other players.

King complained to the president of the United States Lawn Tennis Association (USLTA). All he did was threaten to **suspend** her. King told him the game was so badly run that she didn't care if she played or not.

King continued to speak out. So did other players. Finally, the USLTA and the British Lawn Tennis Association voted to award cash prizes to all winners, whether the players were **amateur** or professional.

Next King began a campaign to award equal prizes to men and women. Men received much greater prize amounts than women did. For example, in 1970, King received $600 for winning the Italian Open. The men's winner got $3,500—nearly six times the amount King won!

To protest the unfair prizes, King decided to start her own tennis tournament. She convinced Virginia Slims cigarettes to

put up the prize money. Then King and nine other women skipped one of the USLTA's events to play in the new Virginia Slims Tournament. This was the first tennis tournament just for women.

The USLTA suspended the women for their actions. But that didn't stop the women.

In January 1971, the Virginia Slims Tournament expanded into the Virginia Slims **Tour**. Twenty-nine tournaments were scheduled that year, with at least $10,000 in prize money for each event. The tour did well. King won 8 of the first 14 tournaments.

In 1972, King won the French Open, the Wimbledon Tournament, and the U.S. Open. That year, *Sports Illustrated* magazine named King its first Sports Person of the Year.

Despite King's hard work and the popularity of women's tennis, many people still believed that women could not be equal to men in sports. One person who said this was tennis player Bobby Riggs.

Riggs was a former Wimbledon champion who loved public **spectacles**. He spent a lot of time bragging about himself and fooling other players into believing they couldn't beat him.

In 1973, Riggs said that no woman could win a match against a man. He challenged King to play him. King refused. She didn't think tennis would be helped by this sort of publicity stunt.

Another woman player, Margaret Court, agreed to play Riggs. Riggs presented her with flowers before the match. Then he distracted Court so much, she lost, 6–2 and 6–1.

When King heard the news, she realized she had to play Bobby Riggs. It no longer mattered how much of a spectacle the match might be.

On September 20, 1973, Bobby Riggs and Billie Jean King entered the Houston Astrodome for the "Battle of the Sexes." The winner would take the $100,000 prize.

Riggs was brought in on a **rickshaw** pulled by several barely dressed women. King was brought in on a **litter** carried by shirtless young men. King went along with the silliness and had fun with the spectacle. But when it came to playing tennis, she was very serious.

Riggs was 55 years old—25 years older than King. Still, most people thought he would win the match.

About 30,000 people watched the match in the Astrodome, and 50 million more watched at home on TV. They saw King soundly defeat Riggs 6–4, 6–3, 6–3. Then she went back to her hotel room and celebrated by ordering "about 30 ice-cream sundaes."

King was happy to have won the match. She was also glad the whole thing was finally over. Most of all, she felt that she had proven that women were just as good—if not better—than men when it came to sports. Young women all over the world now had proof that they could succeed at sports too.

"That match wasn't just about women," King told reporters later. "It was about equal opportunity. A lot of young men who watched that match are today's decision makers. And they think it's normal for their daughters to have equal opportunities with boys. I think that match helped bring that about."

King founded the Women's Tennis Association in 1973. She served as its president.

King continued playing until the early 1980s. She won her last major title in 1980. She and Martina Navritilova won the women's doubles championship at the U.S. Open. King retired in 1983. She was voted into the International Women's Sports Hall of Fame in 1980 and into the International Tennis Hall of Fame in 1987.

In 1990, *Life* magazine named King one of the "100 Most Important Americans of the 20th Century." Only three other athletes made the list, and they were all men.

King remained active in women's tennis even after her days as a player were over. She coached the U.S. Federation Cup team, played on the Virginia Slims Legends Tour, owned a World Team Tennis team, and started the Billie Jean King Foundation to promote equal opportunity outside sports.

"Everything I do is about equal opportunity," she said in a 1998 interview with *Newsweek* magazine. "Race, gender, sexual orientation. Let's get over it. Let's celebrate our differences."

Billie Jean King's Accomplishments

By the time she retired from tennis, Billie Jean King had

- won 20 Wimbledon titles (6 singles, 10 doubles, 4 **mixed doubles**)
- won 4 U.S. Open singles titles, 5 doubles titles, and 4 mixed-doubles titles
- won 2 Australian Open singles championships and 1 mixed-doubles championship
- won 4 mixed-doubles titles at the French Open, as well as 1 singles and 1 doubles title
- helped the U.S. Federation Cup team win seven cups in nine tries by winning 51 of 55 singles and doubles matches
- become the first woman in any sport to earn more than $100,000 in one year (1971)

Jim Abbott

3

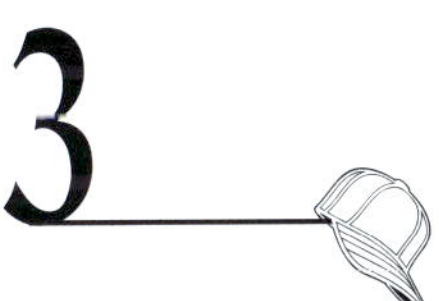

It was September 4, 1993. As Yankee pitcher Jim Abbott threw the last pitch of the game, the crowd went wild. Not only had the Yankees beaten the Cleveland Indians 4 to 0, but Abbott had pitched a **no-hitter**.

Pitching a no-hitter is an exciting moment in baseball. It doesn't happen very often. But this no-hitter was really unique. Jim Abbott had only one hand. He was one of the few professional athletes with a disability. And he was the only disabled player to pitch a no-hitter.

When Jim Abbott was born in Flint, Michigan, on September 19, 1967, his right arm ended at the wrist. His parents were sad that his right hand was missing. But they refused to treat their son differently or allow him to feel sorry for himself. In fact, Abbott's parents always encouraged him to do anything he set his mind to.

When Abbott was five years old, he was fitted with an artificial hand. But he didn't like the way the metal hand looked. When his classmates started calling him names such as "Captain Hook," Abbott stopped wearing the hand. He learned to manage just fine with his one real hand.

One of the things Abbott loved most was sports. He spent many hours playing ball with his father, brother, and friends. When he was 11 years old, he played in the outfield for the local Little League team.

One day, the team's coach announced that he needed a starting pitcher. Everyone was surprised when Abbott volunteered. They were even more amazed when he pitched a no-hitter! After that, Abbott was the team's number-one pitcher.

Usually, a pitcher throws the ball with one hand and wears a fielder's glove on his other hand. Abbott couldn't pitch this way. So, he developed his own style. He rested the pocket of the glove on his right wrist. Then he pitched the ball with his left hand. As soon as the ball was in flight, Abbott slipped his left hand into the glove and was ready to field. After a catch, he tucked the glove under his right arm, grabbed the ball as it fell out of the glove's pocket, then threw it with his left hand. Abbott did all this so fast, fans were hardly able to see what was happening.

During his senior year in high school, Abbott won ten games and lost only three. He also pitched three no-hitters. Abbott was a great hitter too. His batting average was .427, and he hit seven home runs.

Amazingly, Abbott didn't just play baseball. He was also the starting quarterback for his high school football team!

After high school, Abbott turned down a contract with the Toronto Blue Jays. Instead, he attended the University of Michigan on a baseball scholarship.

During his freshman year, Abbott was named to the Big Ten Playoffs All-Tournament Team. This was a tremendous achievement for a freshman.

During his sophomore year, Abbott had an 11–3 record. He pitched 35 straight innings without giving up an **earned run**.

During the summer of 1987, Abbott was the starting pitcher for Team U.S.A. at the Pan-American Games in Cuba. Team U.S.A. won a silver medal. And Abbott won many new fans.

After the Pan-American Games, Abbott decided to become a professional baseball player. But many teams were skeptical about signing a pitcher with only one hand.

The California Angels had no doubts. They signed Abbott in the first round of the 1988 draft. But before he started playing for the Angels, Abbott went to Seoul, Korea, with the U.S. Olympic baseball team. He pitched the team to a gold medal in the final game. Then it was time for him to join the Angels back in the United States.

Most baseball players start their professional careers by playing in the minor leagues for a season or more. It takes time for them to get used to playing major league ball with major-league players. Because of his disability, everyone believed that Jim Abbott would start his career in the minors too.

But Abbott pitched so well during spring training that the Angels decided he was ready for the big time. In April 1989, Abbott was named as a starting pitcher with the California Angels. Only ten other major league pitchers had skipped the minor leagues and gone straight into the majors.

Abbott made his first major league appearance on April 8, 1989. He didn't pitch too well in that game. He allowed six runs in just under five innings. But he soon settled down.

Abbott ended the season with a 12–12 record and 115 strikeouts. Winning 12 games was a great start for any rookie pitcher. In fact, it was one of the best starts an Angels' pitcher had ever had.

By 1991, no one paid much attention to Abbott's missing hand anymore. He had proven that he was just as good a player as anyone else. One newspaper observed that Abbott was no longer being judged by the number of hands he had, but by how he pitched.

In 1991, Abbott had his best season. He ended it with an 18–11 record and a 2.89 **earned run average**. Abbott was considered one of the best pitchers in the game that year.

Fans were stunned when the Angels traded Abbott to the New York Yankees after the 1992 season.

But Abbott enjoyed playing for the Yankees. He was with

the Yankees when he achieved the biggest thrill of his career by pitching the no-hitter against Cleveland in 1993.

Abbott played with the Yankees until 1994. Then he went back to the Angels. Later he played for the Chicago White Sox. But his pitching arm wasn't as good as it had been earlier in his career. In 1997, Abbott retired.

But Jim Abbott wasn't done with baseball yet. He came back as a pitcher with the Chicago White Sox in 1998 and won all five games he started. In 1999, after playing for the Milwaukee Brewers, Abbott retired for the second time.

Jim Abbott never set out to be an inspiration. He just wanted to play baseball. He not only achieved his dream, but he did much more. He proved that the only things that matter in sports are ability and attitude. Abbott was a winner on both counts.

Other Disabled Baseball Players

Jim Abbott may be the most famous disabled baseball player. But he's not the only one. Here are some other baseball notables.

- Mordecai Brown was known as "Three-Finger Brown" after he badly injured his right hand in two childhood accidents. Brown's damaged hand gave him an unusual pitching motion that confused hitters. In 1908, he set a Chicago Cubs' team record when he won 29 games in one season. That record still stands today.

- In 1926, pitcher Grover Cleveland Alexander helped the St. Louis Cardinals win the World Series. He was deaf in one ear and suffered from epilepsy and double vision. Alexander's deafness and epilepsy were the results of his service in World War I. His double vision came from an accident during a minor league game earlier in his career.

- Outfielder Pete Gray played major league baseball for the St. Louis Browns in 1945, despite the fact that he had lost his right arm in a childhood accident. Many people think that Gray would not have played if many baseball players hadn't been overseas serving in the U.S. Armed Forces during World War II. But even though his career was short, Gray became an inspiration to sports fans and wounded war veterans.

- Center fielder Jim Eisenreich played for several different teams during the 1980s and 1990s, despite having a brain disorder called Tourette's syndrome. Eisenreich played in two World Series during his 16-year career.

Janet Guthrie

On May 29, 1977, more than 400,000 fans gathered at the Indianapolis Motor Speedway for the annual Indy 500 auto race. When the owner of the speedway announced the start of the race, the people in the audience heard a historic announcement. "In company with the first lady ever to qualify at Indianapolis—gentlemen, start your engines," the owner said. That day, there was one lone woman among 32 men racing at Indy. That woman's name was Janet Guthrie.

Janet Guthrie was born on March 7, 1938, in Iowa City, Iowa. Her father was an airline pilot. During her childhood, the family moved many times. Guthrie lived in Iowa, New York, Georgia, and Florida.

Guthrie always liked to be on the move. Like other children, she spent a lot of time riding her bicycle around the neighborhood. By the time she was 13, she wanted more excitement than her bike could provide. So she convinced her father to teach her to fly a plane.

When Guthrie was 16, she decided to take up skydiving. To prove to her parents that she wasn't afraid, she jumped off the roof of the Guthries' house. After she'd made a safe landing, her parents agreed she could take skydiving lessons.

Guthrie was always good at science in school. After she graduated from high school, she studied **physics** at the University of Michigan. She also worked as a flight instructor. By the time she graduated, she had spent more than 400 hours in the air and learned to fly 20 different kinds of planes.

After college, Guthrie got a job as an engineer for Republic Aviation in Long Island, New York. In 1965, she heard that the National Aeronautics and Space Administration (NASA) was looking for scientists. NASA planned to train those scientists to be astronauts, who would later travel to the moon.

Going into space sounded wonderful to Guthrie. She took NASA's test and was one of only four women who passed. But she didn't have enough advanced science training to meet NASA's requirements, so she was not chosen.

Guthrie's disappointment over not making it into the space program didn't last long. She had discovered another way to travel.

In 1960, Guthrie had bought a used Jaguar XK-120. She had joined a local car club and had begun competing in **gymkhanas**. These special car races tested a driver's skill. Drivers had to weave in and out of rubber pylons as fast as they could to win. Soon Guthrie was the women's gymkhana champion of Long Island.

Later, Guthrie went to racing school. At racing school, she learned the meanings of different flags that told drivers what the course was like. Guthrie also gained confidence and learned to make daring moves at high speeds. She also learned how to handle emergencies. Soon Guthrie had a special license to race cars.

Guthrie didn't just learn how to race cars. She learned how to take engines apart and put them back together. Guthrie knew that the more she learned about cars and how they worked, the better driver she would be.

During the 1960s, Guthrie entered many races. She usually placed in the top ten, and she almost always finished. Just finishing a race was a big accomplishment. Many drivers were knocked out early because of accidents or mechanical problems.

In 1966, Guthrie was asked to join a women's racing team. The team was sponsored by MacMillan Oil. MacMillan provided the race cars and the **pit crew** to take care of them. The drivers were paid a small amount of money. MacMillan also paid their expenses. Guthrie was happy to join the team. Later that year, Guthrie quit her engineering job to be a full-time race car driver.

For the next nine years, Guthrie struggled to support herself as a driver. She did well in her races. But she had trouble finding a sponsor to pay her **expenses**. All the sponsors Guthrie talked to refused to take a chance on a woman driver. They thought only men could succeed in this sport.

By 1975, Guthrie was one of the most famous sports car drivers in America. Although she was still struggling to find a sponsor, she had a new goal. She wanted to race in the Indianapolis 500. The Indy 500 is the biggest auto race in America. Only the best drivers compete. Guthrie felt sure she could hold her own in the race.

Guthrie had just one problem. She needed a sponsor to give her enough money to buy a special, high-powered car. The cars cost more than $100,000. And no one would sponsor a woman. In fact, everyone thought Guthrie was just looking for publicity. No one believed she actually meant to enter the race.

Then Guthrie got a phone call from a man named Rolla Vollstedt. Vollstedt was planning to enter two cars in the 1976 Indy 500. One car would be driven by Dick Simon. Vollstedt asked Guthrie if she would like to drive the other car. Of course, Guthrie said "Yes!" Vollstedt didn't care that Guthrie was a woman. He just knew that she had an excellent driving record and the skills to be a winner.

Guthrie traveled to Los Angeles to train with Dick Simon and the rest of Vollstedt's crew. After a few months, she entered the Trenton 200 in Trenton, New Jersey. This 200-**lap** race would be Guthrie's first experience competing in a high-powered car. If she did well, she would qualify for the Indy 500.

Many drivers were angry when they heard Guthrie planned to race. One driver, Billy Vukovich, said he'd eat his hat if any woman performed well at Indy. Another driver said he could teach any man on the street how to race. And that man would be better than Guthrie.

Despite the insults and pressure, Guthrie stayed calm. Her only comment was that people should wait to see how she did in the Trenton 200. When one reporter asked her if she was strong enough to handle a race car, Guthrie reportedly snapped back, "I drive the car. I don't carry it."

The Trenton 200 race began with the announcer saying, "Janet and gentlemen, start your engines." Guthrie got off to a good start.

Right after the race started, two drivers dropped out because of engine trouble. One was Billy Vukovich, the driver who had teased Guthrie. Meanwhile, Guthrie raced on.

Guthrie did fine until lap 70 of the race. She skidded on some shredded tire bits on the track. She was able to get her car under control. But then the car stalled. Fortunately, Guthrie got the car started quickly and was able to stay in the race.

But on the 79th lap, the car started making funny noises. Part of the gears had broken. Although she was disappointed, Guthrie knew she had to pull out of the race.

Even though she didn't finish the Trenton 200, Guthrie had proved she could keep up with the other drivers. Best of all, she was accepted into the Indy 500!

Unfortunately, Guthrie's car was not running well in the days before the big race. Rolla Vollstedt tried unsuccessfully to borrow a car from another Indy driver. In the end, Guthrie had to drop out of the race. But before she did, she set the record for the world's fastest closed-course race by a woman—181 miles per hour.

Soon after she dropped out of the Indy 500, Guthrie was offered a chance to race in the Charlotte World 600 stock car race in Charlotte, North Carolina. Stock cars look like regular cars, but they have large, powerful engines.

Guthrie had no trouble qualifying for the World 600. The other drivers were her only problem. Many drivers made it clear she wasn't welcome on the track. Guthrie responded by driving the best she could during practice runs. Soon the criticism stopped. As Guthrie told reporters, "I'm having very little trouble now that I'm giving them a hard time on the racetrack."

Guthrie finished the World 600 in 15th place out of 40 cars. She was the first woman to complete a major stock car race.

Guthrie spent the next year racing stock cars. She finished among the top 12 cars in ten races.

But Guthrie's heart was in Indianapolis. More than anything, Guthrie wanted another chance at the Indy 500. On May 29, 1977, she got it.

Guthrie had a lot of problems during her first Indy race. Her car's engine wasn't working right. She had to pull off the track nine times so her pit crew could work on it. During one of these stops, fuel from her car soaked through Guthrie's racing suit and burned her skin. Finally, after only 27 laps, Guthrie had to pull out of the race because of engine problems.

Guthrie was determined to do better in 1978. But two days before the start of practice sessions for the race, Guthrie broke her wrist playing tennis. She had to learn how to steer and shift gears without putting a lot of pressure on her right hand. Despite this setback, Guthrie was at the starting line when the race began.

This time, everything went well for Janet Guthrie. She finished the race in ninth place and became the first woman to ever complete the Indy 500.

Janet Guthrie opened the door to women at Indy. The May 2000 Indianapolis 500 was the first to have two women entered. Those women were Lyn St. James and Sarah Fisher. Whatever the future holds for women race car drivers, Janet Guthrie led the way.

Lee Elder

5

Tiger Woods is a role model for many young golfers, both on and off the course. But Tiger has his own role models. One of the men he admires most is Lee Elder. Elder was the first black golfer to play in the Masters, one of the most important and exciting golf tournaments.

Lee Elder was born on July 14, 1934, in Dallas, Texas. He came from a large family. Elder was the seventh of eight children. His early childhood was happy and secure.

When the United States entered World War II in December 1941, Elder's father went off to fight. A few months later, he was killed in action.

Mrs. Elder did her best to take care of her large family. But she became sick and died just a few years later. Elder's oldest sister kept the family together. But Elder felt lost, scared, and alone.

Another problem the Elder family faced was money. Elder decided to get a part-time job to help his family. But the only job he could find was **caddying** for golfers at Dallas's Tenison Park. The more he watched the players, the more he wanted to golf himself.

Tiger Woods

One day, Elder went to the park manager and said he wanted to learn to play golf. The manager shook his head. Then he told Elder that blacks were not allowed to play on the course.

Elder was angry. But he refused to give up. Instead, he borrowed an old golf club. Then he picked up golf balls that players had lost on the course. Late at night, when no one was around, Elder sneaked into the park and taught himself to play.

Within a year, Elder was a good golfer, despite the fact that he had never taken a lesson. But there was no place for a black man to play golf in Dallas. So Elder moved to Los Angeles, California, to live with his brother. In California, anyone could play on the public golf courses. Elder was thrilled to be able to take lessons and play every day.

By the time he was a junior in high school, golf was all that mattered to Elder. He decided to quit school and play golf full-time. Although his brother didn't want Elder to leave school, he finally agreed. Elder spent the next few years playing in—and usually winning—tournaments. He also served as captain of the army golf team and taught at a golf course in Washington, D.C.

By the early 1960s, Elder had won ten straight

tournaments in the United Golf Association (UGA). But these victories didn't please Elder as much as they should have.

The UGA was an all-black league. Its cash prizes were very small, and most golf fans hadn't even heard of the organization. It couldn't compare with the Professional Golfers' Association (PGA).

But until 1961, membership in the PGA was limited to whites. After that rule was changed, golfers still had to pass a test, have a high school diploma, and have enough money to support themselves through one year on the tour.

Elder went back to school and saved every penny. Then he took the PGA qualifying tests and placed ninth in his class of 122. Elder was in the PGA!

Elder was a good player. He became very well-known on the PGA tour.

By 1968, Elder was a star. But he also faced a great deal of abuse. Fans taunted him and called him ugly names. Children stole his balls from the course while he played. People told him that he shouldn't be playing a "white" sport.

Despite the difficulties, Elder kept playing. Although he was a star in the PGA, he was never invited to play in the Masters tournament.

The Masters is one of the most challenging and important tournaments in golf. It has been played in Augusta, Georgia, since 1934. For most of the tournament's history, the only way to play in the Masters was to receive an invitation. Elder knew he deserved a chance to compete there. But year after year passed without an invitation to play.

In 1973, eighteen U.S. Congressmen sent a letter to the chairman of the Masters. The letter said that Congress was concerned there were still no blacks competing in the Masters. It went on to urge the chairman to send Lee Elder a special invitation to join the tournament.

When Elder heard about the letter, he said he would refuse an invitation that wasn't based on his abilities. He wanted to play in the Masters because he deserved to, not because he was given special treatment for the color of his skin.

Then, on April 21, 1974, Elder won the Monsanto Open in Pensacola, Florida. The PGA had recently changed its rules so that anyone who won a PGA Tour event would automatically be invited to play in the Masters the following year. Lee Elder had finally made it!

By the time the 1975 Masters began on April 10, Elder had become even more famous. He was on the cover of *Sports Illustrated* and was interviewed by many reporters. When he finally stepped onto the course, he was the only black there, except for the caddies and a few fans. Still, he was determined to enjoy his first Masters appearance.

Halfway through the tournament, golfers who scored over a certain number were eliminated. Sadly, Elder was one of those who didn't make the cut. But he had broken one of golf's toughest barriers and gone into the record books.

Over the next few years, Elder competed in five more Masters' tournaments. In 1979, he had his best Masters performance when he tied for 17th place.

In 1997, Tiger Woods demolished several records when he won the Masters. He was the first black to win, as well as the youngest winner. He also achieved the lowest score in Masters' history.

But Woods did not believe he deserved all the credit for his incredible performance. After he won, Woods told reporters, "I'm the first, but I wasn't the pioneer. Charlie Sifford, Lee Elder, Teddy Rhodes—those guys paved the way for me to be here. I thank them. Because of what they did, I was able to play here."

Charlie Sifford

Lee Elder was an important part of opening the world of golf to blacks. But he wasn't the only one who made a difference. Charlie Sifford was another golf pioneer.

Charlie Sifford was born on June 2, 1922. Like Lee Elder, he learned about golf when he worked as a caddy as a teenager. For most of his career, he was forced to play in minor tournaments because the PGA did not allow blacks to play in its tournaments. That rule was finally dropped in 1961.

That same year, Sifford became the first black golfer to play in a PGA event. The tournament was the Greater Greensboro Open in Greensboro, North Carolina. As he played, Sifford was harassed and insulted by the crowd.

In 1967, Sifford became the first black to win a PGA event. He came in first in the Greater Hartford Open in Hartford, Connecticut. He continued to play until 1971 and finished in the top 60 for lifetime earnings.

After his retirement from golf, Sifford started a foundation to introduce golf to black children and inner-city youths. He hopes to give these children the opportunity to make a difference in the sport he loves.

Getting Around the Ban

In January 1952, Bill Spiller, Ted Rhodes, and Eural Clark became the first black golfers to play in a big-name golf tournament when they entered the Phoenix Open in Phoenix, Arizona. They were able to play because the PGA had recently passed a rule that allowed black players to enter if the tournament's sponsor said it was okay.

Manon Rheaume

6

The action on the ice is fast and furious at a professional hockey game. The puck zooms back and forth across the ice. Sticks smack against one another. Players push and shove as they try to control the puck. Standing in the net, the goalie lunges across the ice, smacking the puck away to make **save** after save.

Then the game ends and the goalie pulls off the protective mask and helmet. Imagine the crowd's surprise when they see who was playing the position. Although all the other players are men, the goalie is a young woman!

Manon Rheaume was that young woman. She was the first woman to play professional hockey on a men's team. But that moment was just one of the exciting breakthroughs this dedicated hockey player has accomplished during her career.

Manon Rheaume was born on February 24, 1972. She grew up in Lac Beauport, a suburb of Quebec City, Canada. Everyone in the Rheaume family loved sports.

Quebec City, Canada

Rheaume's father flooded the backyard so Rheaume and her two brothers could skate there during the winter. She was zipping around the ice by the time she was three years old. She loved guarding the net while her brothers took shots at her.

Rheaume's father also coached a local boys' hockey team. One day when she was five, her father announced his team needed a goalie for a local tournament. Rheaume had plenty of experience playing goalie with her brothers, so she volunteered. From that day, Rheaume was hooked on hockey.

Rheaume played on boys' hockey teams while she was growing up. She often faced difficulties winning a spot on the teams, simply because she was a girl. At first, all the coaches and players laughed at her. But once they saw her talent and determination, they wanted her on the team.

When Rheaume was 11, she tried out for the Quebec International Peewee Tournament. Rheaume had dreamed about playing in this competition, and she worked hard to win a spot. She believed that she deserved to be on the top level AA team. Instead, she was cut from AA and placed on the CC team. According to Rheaume's father, the AA coach believed that no girl could handle the pressures of playing hockey, so he refused to have a girl on his team.

Even though she was disappointed, Rheaume played hard for the CC team. "They may think they're going to stop me, but I've wanted to play . . . for as long as I can remember, and I will," she was reported to have said. With Rheaume tending goal, the CC team made it to the semifinals of the 1983–84 world championship.

Although Rheaume loved playing hockey and clearly had a lot of talent, many coaches and parents didn't want her to play. They felt that she was taking a place that rightfully belonged to a boy. A boy might have a chance to play in the National Hockey League (NHL). Why waste a team spot on a girl who never would make it to the NHL?

Rheaume also faced difficulties because of her size. Many hockey players are tall and heavy. But she was only five feet, six inches tall and weighed about 135 pounds. However, goalies rely more on skill and speed than they do on size and strength. That meant Rheaume's small size was not as much of a disadvantage as it would have been if she played a different position.

By the time she was 17, Rheaume was playing for Canada's Midget AA league. But most of the other players weren't as dedicated to hockey as she was. And she still faced a lot of resentment and anger from coaches and fans. Rheaume needed a break. She stopped playing hockey and went to college. But she missed hockey too much to stay away.

In 1991, Rheaume's brother Pascal tried out for the Trois-Riviere's Draveurs, which was one level below the NHL. Rheaume was asked to try out too.

Pascal made the Draveurs. Rheaume joined their **second-string** team, the Louiseville Jaguars. She also played backup goalie for the Draveurs. Rheaume was the first woman to reach this high level in hockey.

On November 26, 1991, Rheaume finally got a chance to fill in for the Draveurs' goalie. She played 17 minutes and stopped 13 of 16 shots. Then a puck hit her mask and sliced open her left eyebrow. Rheaume had to leave the game to get the cut stitched up.

Rheaume never got another chance to play for the Draveurs. But lots of people had noticed her in that one game. Suddenly, she was one of the

hottest stories in sports.

Phil Esposito was one of the people who heard about Rheaume's accomplishment. During the 1960s and 1970s, Esposito had been a star hockey player with the NHL's Chicago Blackhawks, Boston Bruins, and New York Rangers. In 1992, he was the general manager of the Tampa Bay Lightning, a new NHL team.

Esposito invited Rheaume to join the Lightning at training camp. Esposito wanted to give Rheaume a shot at playing in the NHL. He also thought that having her at camp would create a lot of interest in his team. Rheaume was eager for a chance to play and quickly accepted Esposito's offer.

Twenty-year-old Rheaume had no trouble keeping up with the men at training camp. On September 23, 1992, Tampa Bay played an **exhibition game** with another NHL team, the St. Louis Blues.

Esposito decided it was time to give Rheaume her big chance. He put her in as goalie during the first period of the

game. During those 20 minutes, Rheaume blocked seven of nine shots.

After the exhibition game, Esposito told reporters, "There are not many 20-year-olds, men or women, who can play goal in the NHL, especially those who haven't had the experience. She has God-given talent." Then Esposito signed Rheaume to a contract with the Lightning's minor-league team, the Atlanta Knights.

On December 3, 1992, while playing with the Knights, Rheaume became the first woman to play in a regular season professional hockey game. Rheaume later played on several other minor league men's teams.

Manon Rheaume has also been active on the Canadian women's hockey team. She was Canada's goaltender at the 1992 International Ice Hockey Federation (IIHF) Women's World Championship. During the championship, she gave up just two goals in three games, and Canada won the gold medal.

Rheaume also helped the Canadian women's hockey team win the 1994 IIHF Women's World Championship. And she played goalie on Canada's women's hockey team during the 1998 Winter Olympics in Nagano, Japan. Canada came home with a silver medal from Nagano, which was the first Olympics to feature women's ice hockey.

Rheaume also plays roller hockey. In 1996, she achieved another historic "first" while playing for the Sacramento River Rats of the Roller Hockey International (RHI) league. She was the first female goalie to defeat a male goalie in an RHI game.

Whether it's professional hockey, Olympic hockey, or roller hockey, Manon Rheaume has proven that she has what it takes to succeed. And she's shown everyone that it doesn't matter whether you're a male or a female, as long as you have the will.

Another Hockey Pro

In 1993, Erin Whitten became the first U.S. woman to play professional hockey. She has tended goal for several NHL minor league teams.

THE WNBA

Rebecca Lobo and Sheryl Swoopes

7

The fans gathered in New York's Madison Square Garden were watching a thrilling basketball game. But the game wasn't being played by the New York Knicks, the city's National Basketball Association (NBA) team. It was being played by the New York Liberty, a team made up entirely of women.

Similar scenes were taking place in Los Angeles, Houston, Phoenix, Cleveland, and other U.S. cities. The Women's National Basketball Association (WNBA) was here! And it had been a long road for women to finally have the chance to play in the big leagues.

Basketball was invented in 1891 by a physical education teacher named James Naismith. In 1892, the game was modified so women could play. A few years later, the rules for women's basketball were published, and the sport spread around the country.

In those days, the women's game was called *basquette*. It was very different from the men's game! Basquette players stayed in certain areas of the court during the game. They did not run all over the way the men did. The women's game was much less physical than the men's game. And it was shorter. The reason the rules were different was that in those days people thought women were weak and couldn't stand too much exercise.

In the 1930s, a team called the All-American Red-Heads traveled around the country. The Red-Heads not only played by the men's rules, they played men's teams. The women players didn't want anyone to forget they were female. So they played in full makeup and wore bright red wigs!

Several important events affected women's basketball during the 1970s. The first big change occurred in 1971. The rules were changed to allow women to play the same five-player, full-court game the men played. Now the games looked identical.

President Richard Nixon

In 1972, President Richard Nixon signed Title IX of the Educational Amendment. Title IX stated that no one could be discriminated against in sports because of gender. Schools had to provide the same opportunities for women's sports as they did for men's.

Slowly, girls began to play the same sports as boys. They won athletic scholarships to colleges. Teams made up of both boys and girls popped up in schools and communities around the country. And everyone began to take the idea of women playing sports more seriously.

In July 1976, women's basketball made its first Olympic appearance at the Summer Games in Montreal, Canada. The U.S. won the silver medal. One of the team's players was 18-year-old Nancy Lieberman. She became the youngest basketball player in Olympic history to win a medal.

By the late 1970s, women were hungry for opportunities to play professional basketball. In 1978, the Women's Professional Basketball League (WBL) was formed. But the league only had eight teams. It shut down after just three seasons.

Ann Meyers-Drysdale, left, and Jackie Stiles, right

In 1979, college star Ann Meyers signed a one-year contract with the NBA's Indiana Pacers. She was invited to the Pacers' training camp, but she didn't make the team. Part of the problem may have been her size. Meyers was five feet, nine inches tall. That's tall for a woman. But it's pretty short for a professional basketball player!

During the 1980s, women's basketball saw many firsts. The U.S. women's basketball team won its first gold medal at the Summer Olympics in Los Angeles, California, in 1984. That same year, the first women were **inducted** into the Basketball Hall of Fame.

In 1985, Lynette Woodard became the first woman to play for the Harlem Globetrotters. The Globetrotters are a team that shows off its amazing basketball skills in exhibition games around the country.

Then, in 1986, Nancy Lieberman became the first woman to play in a professional men's league. She joined the Springfield Fame of the United States Basketball League (USBL). The following year, Lieberman joined the Washington Generals. This team tours with the Globetrotters. Lieberman was their first female player.

In spite of these few high-publicity events, women who wanted to play professional basketball didn't have many opportunities. The best U.S. players had to join European teams if they wanted to play professionally. That meant leaving home, family, and friends and learning a new language. They also had to get used to new customs and foods. There simply was nowhere to play professionally in the United States.

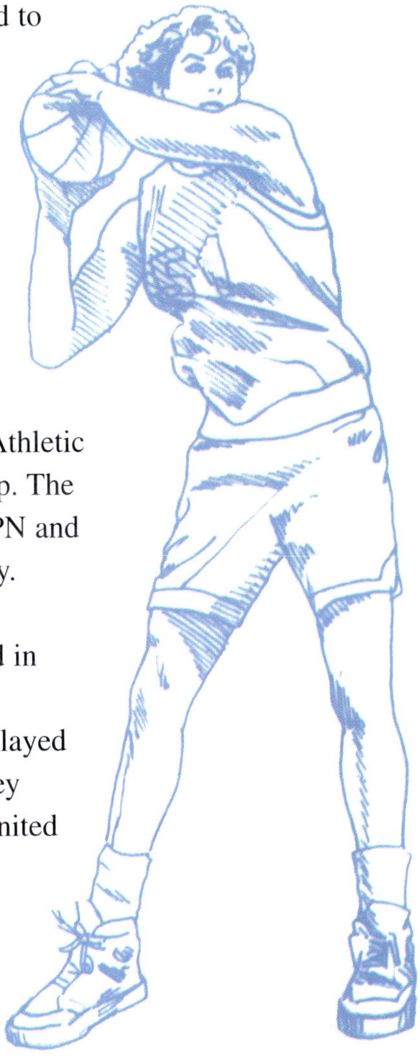

Everything began to change in 1995. That year, the University of Connecticut women's basketball team, the Huskies, won all 35 of its games. The Huskies went on to win the 1995 National Collegiate Athletic Association (NCAA) championship. The NCAA game was televised on ESPN and thrilled viewers all over the country.

The USA Basketball Women's National Team was also introduced in 1995. This team spent 14 months traveling around the world. They played in Asia, Europe, and Australia. They also played college teams in the United States. The team ended up with an undefeated 52–0 record. The team went on to represent the United States at the 1996 Summer Olympics in Atlanta, Georgia.

Members of the U.S. Women's 1996 Olympic Basketball Team. From left to right are: Jennifer Azzi, Ruthie Bolton, Teresa Edwards, Venus Lacey, Lisa Leslie, Rebecca Lobo, Katrina McClain, Nikki McCray, Carla McGhee, Dawn Staley, Katy Steding, and Sheryl Swoopes.

They won all of their games there and came home with a gold medal. For the first time, there seemed to be enough interest in the United States for a women's basketball league to succeed.

The months following the 1996 Olympics saw the formation of not one, but two professional women's basketball leagues. The first was the American Basketball League. Although the level of play was excellent in the ABL, the league could not compete with the other women's basketball league. When the ABL folded in 1998, many of its players joined the other league. That league was the WNBA, which was part of the NBA.

When the WNBA started playing in 1997, the league had eight teams. Those teams were the Houston Comets, the New York Liberty, the Charlotte Sting, the Cleveland Rockers, the Phoenix Mercury, the Los Angeles Sparks, the Sacramento Monarchs, and the Utah Starzz. The women who made up these teams were the stars of the 1996 Olympic team. Old favorites such as Lynette

Woodard and Nancy Lieberman also came out to play in the WNBA.

Later, the league expanded several times. By the 2000 season, the WNBA included the original eight teams, plus the Washington Mystics, the Detroit Shock, the Minnesota Lynx, the Orlando Miracle, the Miami Sol, the Portland Fire, the Seattle Storm, and the Indiana Fever.

Fans loved the WNBA. The teams drew huge crowds to their games. Millions more fans watched the games on TV. Players such as Rebecca Lobo, Teresa Weatherspoon, Cynthia Cooper, and Sheryl Swoopes became superstars. Some people even preferred the WNBA to the NBA. They said that the women's games featured better ballhandling and sharper skills.

Most importantly, the WNBA gave women basketball players a chance to make a living playing the game they loved. And they didn't have to travel halfway around the world to do it. The men had been doing that for years. Now it was the women's turn!

Cynthia Cooper, left, and Teresa Weatherspoon, right

Still a Different Game

Although the women in the WNBA play basically the same game as the men in the NBA, there are a few differences. The baskets are the same height—10 feet. But the ball is 29.5 inches around in the WNBA. It's 30 inches in the NBA. This difference allows for women's smaller hands. WNBA games are 40 minutes long, which is 8 minutes shorter than NBA games. The **shot clock** is 30 seconds in the WNBA and 24 seconds in the NBA. The **three-point line** is 4 feet closer to the basket in the WNBA. The lane down the middle of the court is 4 feet narrower than the lane in the NBA.

Glossary

amateur	someone who takes part in a sport for fun rather than for money
antagonize	to cause anger
barrier	something that blocks progress
caddy	to help a golfer with his or her clubs and often give advice about the course
discharge	release or dismissal from service
discrimination	act of treating someone differently based on race, gender, etc., rather than on ability
doubles	game of tennis with two players on each side of the net
earned run	in baseball, a run scored without any errors being committed
earned run average	in baseball, the average number of earned runs the pitcher allows in a game
exhibition game	practice game that is played before the public, usually before the regular season starts
expenses	cost of maintaining a business
gender	sex, such as male or female
gymkhana	special car race that tests a driver's skills and agility

induct	to admit as a member
integrate	to end segregation (see glossary entry) by bringing together as equals
lap	in racing, one time around the track
league	group of teams that play against one another
litter	covered and curtained couch on a platform that is carried on the shoulders of four or more people
mixed doubles	game of tennis with two players—one man and one woman—on each side of the net
no-hitter	in baseball, a game in which the pitcher does not allow the other team to get any hits
obstacle	something that stands in the way of progress or success
petition	formal written request
physics	science that deals with matter and energy and how they interact
pit crew	in auto racing, the people who refuel and repair a car during the race
professionally	for money
rickshaw	small covered two-wheeled vehicle for one passenger that is pulled by people

rookie	athlete who is in his or her first season with a professional (see glossary entry) team
save	act of preventing the other team from scoring
scholarship	money that pays for someone to go to college
second-string	being the substitute for the regular team
segregate	to separate or set apart because of differences
shot clock	in basketball, a clock that measures how much time a team has to shoot at the basket
singles	game of tennis with one player on each side of the net
spectacle	entertaining, often outrageous, public event
suspend	to take away a privilege or membership
taunt	mock in an insulting manner; ridicule
three-point line	line on a basketball court; shots taken from behind that line are worth three points
tour	in golf or tennis, a series of professional tournaments
tournament	athletic competition having several rounds or games

Index